THE BLUE CAT

By F. D. Reeve

The Brother, *novel*
Just over the Border, *novel*
The Red Machines, *novel*
In the Silent Stones, *poems*
Robert Frost in Russia
The Russian Novel
Aleksandr Blok: Between Image and Idea

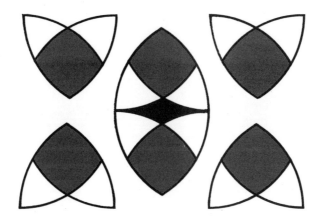

The Blue Cat

poems by

F D Reeve

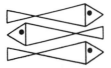

FARRAR, STRAUS AND GIROUX

NEW YORK

"Opus aestivum," "The Long Trail," "A Seaside Crucifix," "Hands,"
"Hope," and "Last Game for the New Life" originally appeared in
Poetry. Other poems originally appeared in *The Tin Drum,
Focus/Midwest, The Little Magazine,*
and *Unmuzzled Ox.*

CONTENTS

PRESENTS & DISSENTS

A Weel

A spider falls dazzled
by sunlight
by its own web-spinning
into the fork of the hawthorn.
Helen, her head resting
in my elbow dividers,
opens her lips
for a grape.
Ten long-legged shadows lie
across the façade
of the south elevation.

In the cellar
of the mind
ten bottles lie
in redemptive darkness,
on each a spider
riding westward
patiently quoining
a distant façade,
the reddendum,
where children play in the rooms
like shadows.

Yesterday
a yellow spider
captured the kitchen table.
It followed the bottles

3

into the doorway,
tied the legs to the floor,
the arms to the legs,
bound eyes and lips,
then changing its mind,
rising after its fall,
coming back to itself,
resumed resurrection.
Watch it in the sunlight
weave the next web.

Sea-leavings

October winds upset the water.
The current runs west into the waves.
Thin fingers of spume, Daughter,
touch the soft hair on your face.

Watch the fish die in the dirty river.
Cheap alive, they stink dead.
Aquarius carries; who was the giver?
You have a lover, as others have had

spring and summer, before the water
turned on itself, the green moon
expired, like grass, in black laughter,
and the edge of the sea fell into the sun.

The keel carves its cold secrets,
whom it loves on its silent course
through weeds and ice, hanging like a locket
at the round white throat of the earth.

Like pregnant women in corkscrew motion
the dying fish swim into the air.
The end comes slowly in this troubled season
as the salt water dries on your gold hair.

Hands

for Paul Horgan

How straight and modest is the arc-subtending mind.
It lifts a heavenly arch above flat-bottomed earth
and in the Sistine Chapel prowls the floor behind
the painter waiting for the vault to ripen. Worth
length or radians, it hovers near the center
of the iron world melting in ambiguities
while a Great Circle skirts its small diameter.

When I was a boy I read how perspicuity
of discourse cleared the mind to crystal like a fishbowl.
There were roses, also, on the table. One day I stole
the round blue globe and took it to my darker self
up the black back stairs. I split it with a knife.
The bears and books screamed down from their Olympic shelf
as in my new blue hat I stomped the fallen half.

Like ribs around my body this armillary sphere
cages the fancy with old bars new Marco Polos
must unbend. The heart of the dying sky is kept in here.
Outside, upheld by fission, rolling in sunlight still,
the earth is the moon's lover and follows its dark ways.
Hands float in space around my careless life: Craft says
they might come back; the mind knows they never will.

6

A Seaside Crucifix

for Elizabeth & William McPherson

The sun takes up a geographic post
    each noon which on the buttons of His eyes
    reflected blinds the westbound viking host.
  Cut by iron ships, the ocean dies.

The phosphorescent stars on a winter night
    like frozen sparklers on pendragons' mail
   herald the wounds and sea-deep firelight
as a mast bespeaks the glory of its sail.

One midnight burst of immortality
    drives the sun round to raise the nightwrecked day,
    though each noon fix is fiction. In actuality
Morz est Rollant e li quens Oliver.

His hands reach out for sea-room from His fear.
    In spring, as earth unbandages, His youth
    drips from His bottled body into the green year,
and sailors leap each Sunday from His mouth.

Noon

for Helen & Anthony Hecht

The sun stops in the sky.
  A pair of yellow shoes
  floats in noon delight
      across Delancey Street
         under a skirt of love.

Woe to white women
  who one by one slip
      from the clouds.
         Mourning doves
      sing like waterfalls.

My girl is a ripe meadow.
  She sways in the wind of love
      while old women's hands
         thread her cranberry eyes.

Here, Apollo. This time
  I'm drunk under a white ash.
  Today a yellow girl
      with hips bent like a rainbow
         leapt over my legs.

  Her naked body
      dived to joy,

then rose like a kite
        on her white hair
                entangling the wind.

        I pulled down her knees,
        and they pressed my eyes.

Spring Stars

Here, take my hand.
The white dogwood covers our heads.
Let my thoughts dress your body
          in waking / walking.

Yellow words in the garden
burst from the bulbs of the dead.
Let my fingers inflame your body
          to waking / walking.

Surrender. King Arcas
doomed her: Callisto bled
to death. Let our bodies
          keep waking / walking.

Rats eat dry kingdoms.
Stars rust. The current that led
my hand to your body
          is waking / walking.

Opus aestivum

for Rosmarie & Keith Waldrop

Birds fill the air with brutal
music, not as in the mind
Bach's Fourth Concerto roils the nerve ends
but in and of itself, in kind:
      Leather fingers of a girl
    make love on a harpsichord;
      water falling in the mountains
    wears away the stones.

Nature is loud. Its vulgarities linger
on the ear's edge. In a conch you hear
sharks eating fish in a hollow sea
and birds beating timpani of clouds.
      After a summer storm has passed
    and the clarinet wind is rising,
      voices in the leaves repeat
    the thunder to the grass.

The Long Trail

for Eleanor & Robert Penn Warren

A boy runs through the woods as through his father's mind,
past birch and beech, trillium and lady's-slipper,
past lovers in shadow and losses asleep in wet bogs,
frightening small lies by his pounding feet,
coming to rest on a height by a tall oak where his panting
bellows the news of his life to the rising wind.

Modicum, et vos videbitis me, she said
who, clad in green and red, so well discerned
the cause from the effect that she herself
was the model of God's love drawing
him down the long descent and up to find the stars
fixed, like his father, in the perfect end.

A hawk in a dream is perpetual motion parked
in eccentric circles above a forest path.
No man awake has said to what or why it moves.
Like a boy he looks through the islands of leaves
and remembers that he, too, was Phaëthon
when Zeus, to save the world, struck him dark.

Fire

for Elizabeth & Robert Valkenier

No, not even burnt houses astonish my eyes,
which fatten on darkness. Spotted cows in a meadow
pattern the rural life. An orchard
waits by the roadside; its apples shrink like old men.
Woodsmoke flavors the lingering saffron skies.

Our childhood loves burn like houses. They lean on their walls
under empty winter trees beseeching the birds
for favors. The wind is cold music.
The doors swing on two decades of loneliness;
the losses build their nests in the unheated halls.

Houses have eyes. When flames shoot up the face
and boil off the blood inside, the shutters draw over,
as a girl at the climax closes her eyes.
    If I saw a girl asleep in a meadow of lilies,
    I would lie down beside that burned place.

Mirror Images

for Kate & John Berryman

There in the dirt an old man lies.
      His flesh turns pine, his bones turn lead.
      His regular rhythms are dead.
   His widow stares through fingers of stone
        like her horse's eyes
          hitched on the other side of the road.

A cloud of dust conceals the road
      that splits the village in half ahead.
      Tiger cats flash red
to frighten the family dog to death
      who shakes at the load
        dumped in the gutter of the earth.

A dead man rectifies the earth;
      hope, like salt, stains his bed;
      his fingers break stone bread.
Three sons cross the crest of his road,
        two black from birth
        and one with eyes in the back of his head.

The Rewinding

for Kit & Joseph Reed

The End.
Reverse.
        The frames spin back.
          The spring on the mousetrap rises.
          The head on the twisted neck
            returns to its lost free will.
              The walls stiffen, seal their cracks.
              The house levels out on the sills.
              The hand leaps backward.
              Eyes shut the door.
              The broken sunlight
                flies up from the floor.

Mate

The list is long: Each one crawls to confess
    hatred and self-doubt, the fake assurance
of the early morning departure, the false address
    for forwarding urgent mail
              and appeals
              to come home,
      the final unscrupulous jape of lying to the press
        that the difficulties are beyond human endurance.

The ranks are marked; every player, numbered.
    The knight's adulteries promote himself.
The bishop bleeds his sheep to slow their rumbles.
    The unwashed urban poor
              bare
              their teeth
      at the wall of *flics*. Paving stones and broken lumber
      batter alike Ghibelline and Guelph.

Played with passionate mind, this imported game
    scorches cities and spreads like blight to the green
chestnuts of Ohio and up the Missouri, maiming
    good, bad, white, black,
              rook,
              and pawn—
      Flesh rots off the last impaled name
      until on a hot square of sand in Death Valley
      a naked king screws the dead queen.

Noise

for Edward Williamson

See proud Chanticleer on his morning strut,
flashing green feathers at every low-hung slut.
Up her skirt! He swings his wattle and balls
into victory at sunrise.

                    Down the dawn-filled halls
of Versailles Louis Quatorze returns to his room.
The invisible door to Marie is closed. The loom
is working again. The guards are waking and washing.

Nobody finished the plot, foresaw the squashing
of beasts or the charred timbers of the burned barn.

Look, the woman who wove has bought new yarn.
Down the hall I hear the door to the girl's room creaking.
The cock crows. All the hens are shrieking.

Hope

for Peter Boynton

On the avenue the faces change each day,
    washed like white pebbles on the sand.
  The undertow rolls them. Some must swim away

to form new coral islands. Some swarm, like bees,
    around a silver monarch building an empire
  from the mouth of the Amazon to the Hebrides.

But most, like friends, are turned by the water's care
    into smooth round stones that harden as they grow old,
  etched with error and excessive wear.

They bear their burdens sadly, for they bear them long.
    They barter scars of tragedies for fears
  although, like old religions, all prove wrong.

From this coarse commerce a lover picks by day
    what he can. His hand in his pocket smiles that one
  white stone remains when the rest are washed away.

The Man in the Moon

for Joan Jurale

Father, no. Drop your disguise.
Tears wash the mountains of the moon
    down the winter of its eyes.

Pale circus clowns with red balloons
explode the laughter trapped inside,
    new tricks to satisfy dark moons.

Owls like girls in moonlight glide
through woods of men in love until
    crows tat the bodies on the morning side.

Whose brown bone hands pick out a will
from that dry surface? The dinosaur-
    imprinted seas are cold and still.

White movies in the heavens star
the strawberry lovers you did in.
    My memory kisses their mouths. From far

away their voices shout through long, tin
horns, "Death will be soon,"
    but I don't care. Love is not sin.

Stop. You sing a false tune.
Take off your arms, lips, penis, eyes.
    I am the real man in the moon.

Melancholia

How can you endure the cold in your high castle of kept
Pride, the demesne of Virtue? Darkening worms accept
Winter, sinking under the frozen moat to their first state.
Even dogs bark at the night. The castellan by the gate
Reverences the impatient guest who arrives covered with frost.
     O bitter winter: New lady born, old lover lost.

Fervid heartbeats knock apart the towers of a life.
The handkerchief of love falls down; then Iago's knife
Peels the skin from the flesh. The heart is black; the
                             eyes are stones.
Naked children dance in the empty fosse, ignoring the bones
Of Cenozoic animals, kissing the skulls of form
     With gardenia lips that float from their mouths to the
                             moonlit storm.

Selves must join series. No house of stone will last forever,
Nor this ice. The earth will burn to ash in the sun's weather.
Nothing beyond is predicted. You, too, will fossilize:
First, your breasts will stiffen; then childhood caves will
                             materialize;
On the second day of spring you will flee your room like a
                             harried bootlegger,
     But the dog in the yard will bite at your heels as at
                             those of a passing
                             beggar.

A Cup of Coffee

for James Merrill

The instant world
dissolves at night:
Snake eyes
from the ceiling
hang down
on rubber cords
in the viscid sea;
noses
like suction cups
cling to
her iron spine;
ears, thighs
flip-flop
in the great eddy,
whorling,
cooling
the fingers,
centrifuging
sand dollars,
family cameos,
the bacteria
that by day
rise
in the fluid
of her passions.
Two breasts
bobble
in slow circles,

21

burst one
then two—
slowly
she sinks,
the steel body
slides
shoulder-down
into the black water;
the pale fish
melt like sugar
and are left
on the bottom
like sand.

Last Game for the New Life

for Anne & Mahlon Pitney

Four florid faces: He haunts himself
bidding against mortality. Who else
would willingly finesse a king always
imagining in Paradise fair play?

Men hold hands brutally, at each turn
yielding deuce or trey, brandishing trump.
Wicked the partner who fails to reach the high;
most wicked gravity, the pull of earth.

Around and round, the red and black lie down,
each figure giving/taking toward an end
looping the stars. As luck will have it, some
boomerang tomorrow; some sink with the sun.

You whose face before me like a card
shuffles in ambiguities once said
you would not play this game. Yes, you declined
North South East West to be refined

by hands of fire. You were, you swore, your face.
Sorry: Among the cards you have lost your place,
and your cry here does not start my tears
who, taught to make book, have bid the vulnerable years.

Rubbings

for Ellen & Russell D'Oench

Conspicuously present the dead
from their stone-roofed box-houses
    wink messages, chant morals.

Advice collects in gutters;
coins, in a beggar's cup.
    The letters rub off; the morals

cost too much to keep up.
We couple in fiberglass beds
    bitching about loose morals

and the wind-shaken attic shutter
that bangs like an empty cup:
    Home repairs, street morals.

On the back of a sunken chair
a stone sun rises.
    Its paper face looks moral,

but rubbings have no morals.
No one asks at the door,
    What are they going to do?
                the dead.

The Prepared Voice

Who said the night is silent?
   From the plastic radio
a rubber girl sings wildly
   I love you so.

Her short-hemmed legs explode;
   her eye tubes glow;
the darkness amplifies her
   I love you so.

Slow music smokes the ceiling;
   curved words, like bats, dip low.
Sure, every night, believe me,
   I love you so.

Enchased by morning plucking
   the petals Yes and No,
the mirror frames the echo:
   I love you so.

I Have Just Received a Review of ———, and

I'm challenged to make a poem
    1.   because I am a) ☐ ———
                             b) ☐ ———
              (Fill in the blanks)
              (Your personal choice)
              (10% off for cash)
    2.   because there is a lot of shit in the world
                     a) ☐ True
                     b) ☐ False
    3.   because nobody else has
                     a) ☐ Something to fill in the blanks with
                     b) ☐ The same opportunity
but I'm not going to do it.
Of course, I'm certain that
                     a)
                     b)   THIS SPACE FOR
                             OFFICE USE ONLY

so I'll nick you all, you
                     a) ☐ ———
                     b) ☐ ———
                     c) ☐ Other
        IF
      you'll
       admit
        you're
        not
         so

p
  o
    i
      s
        o
          n
            o u s   a s   f i r s t   a p p e a r e d,

then we can do business:

        a) ☐
        b) ☐

In China I'm a barbarous moth.
I defecate on candles.
      I blackmail windowpanes.
    I fornicate in the cellars of slanted chimneys.
         Yes? No?
It must be an expression of personal opinion.

    Check.

Love Affairs

Gold ferns
an oak
laced air
a Spanish castle
hoofs on stones
pigeons fly up
cold light falls
from your hands
Miranda

Wind overturns leaves
a falcon lifts air in its wings
the river darkens
pause
fire
the rocks explode
relics scream from the floor
in churches of silence
I have forgotten
and remember
the turpentine sunlight
soaks your shirt
the ivory sails whisper
behind the horses
in my tower

Spring returns birds
claws the stones

hand over hand
loving
the old hunters
domestic
apple-red blood
a gored bull
streams down my back
lunging
a gasoline rainbow
to the ultimate
the achieved castle
of your hands

Old maids on a gray veranda
gossip about shoulders
girlhood castles
broken ferns
the overdue hunter
nightgowns
bedpans
I have forgotten
the toothed leaves
the wooden horses
the sailor's snapshot
in the leftover silence

Paper bodies
dissolve
pigeons
swim through the leaves

the castle falls
on its hands

The eye of the lighthouse
opens its gown.

The Revenant of Red Square

Here you see the room he lived in,
  the blotter, bathrobe, comb, brush, jar:

Here we have the barn he hid in,
  froze in his form to fool the Tsar:

Here he lies for all to see him,
  paraffined by parabolist Death:

The Leader lives, but in this museum
  paranoiacs suck the dead man's breath.

The Dragons' Teeth

for William Meredith

Foreign troops in a wheatfield outside Prague
remind me: Seven stalks in Thebes once raised
their plumèd crowns when no rain fell. An amazed
city fought those dogs with staffs and stones.

Bodies rotted on the rocky ground. Crows
and ants banked piles of maggoty eyes.
Drunk, stinking survivors thundered
for souvenirs into the women's wombs.

The sun clawed the guts of the land.
The loins bled, died. The moon embalmed
it. Hushed in Roman darkness a man crept down
to avenge the dragons with his bloodstained hand.

Guernica

for Ernest Simmons

O heiliges neunzehntesjahrhundert,
    white as Clara Schumann's shoulders
    striped like a barber pole with blood
under the hard blue hat of revolution
      and the common good,

whose ideas tunneled through the sand
    of Napoleon's mouth while leg-ironed ants
    scoured the palace floor for food
and *The Beagle* verified the evolution
      of the common good,

give us advice in middle age:
    Whom must the queen take for a lover?
    Do our young men die when they should?
    Will the scarf of war tighten on the neck of the nation
      for the common good?

THE ANTHILL

The Anthill

1

Old women in black hoods
shuffle in to pray for the dead.
(Ants store grain in special ground.)
Jesus rips his hands
free from the nails to touch their loins.
See where his blood has soaked the wood?
They kiss it. They press their cheeks against
the warm brown stains.
                 When infidels flooded
the fields and washed away the grain,
this white house of God, besieged,
shot up a brighter flame.
One spring the roof fell in;
Heaven itself shouldered the rain
until the cross rose higher still.
When Indians attacked, the pastor named
his flock "The Soldiers of God's Will."

Winter huts, like saints in shrouds,
await the Easter resurrection.
Beggars crawl on hands and knees
around the relics of the nation.
Three shadows rise like crumpled bats,
three black-faced girls with outstretched hands
whirling up the groin of Heaven.
Across the floor in single file
the ants transport their packs of sin,

The Church was the center of New England life.

The Church was the leader of society.

Plimouth Colony experienced a double fate.

The Fates forever reenact mortality.

37

weeping freely toward the grail
filled with their loneliness. A sudden
silence blanks the wooden walls;
the wine boils up; and fear walks in.

2

At his birth who were present remarked
the oblong head, the spatulate fingers
instinctually weaving the smoky air;
praised John and Cynthia for a second son
to be a maker of pencils:
With his father's pencils he ruled the land,
"one of the finer American minds"
who took his time, like his people, in hand.
His ghost hangs on the wall:
As the winter fire dies down
and the winds blow across Walden Pond,
a hundred thousand men buy
seeds and sails, call for self-reliance,
and dream of a solitary empire
saluted by the red, morning sun.

With his father's pencils Henry David
has drawn circles around them, friends,
the forty-four stations of his life:
He left nothing to lament.

3

Father, fornicator, release me.
Ille vim tulit invitae.
Aut mihi redde meos

aut me quoque conde sepulchro.
Of my spare years what have I saved
that will free me in the city?
Saints beach icons in the spray
at Sandy Hook. Pity
drags the Fifth Avenue bus.
A thousand immigrants each Fourth of July
wash garbage, hoe water.
Convicted scholiast, once I
wanted Sewall's daughter,
wanted to bed a perfumed lady.
As a river, turned from its course,
ravages its way to the sea, so I braid
my career with what she refused.
My body is bad; that woman's, worse:
She sparrows on brick words,
mindlessly foraging; love is a curse
in her dirty stone dead woods.
Hesper in the transcendent sky,
suck my hot eye.

> The more Thoreau saw New York, the worse he thought it.

> Ellen Sewall's father prevented her marrying one of those radical transcendentalists.

4

Flames from the pine stump
      finger Fair Haven Pond:
Three hundred acres, six
      dressed trout burn.
Shamans slay the tinder
      with orange tongues;
witches devour wood;
      demons dare

> Thoreau was careless with a campfire; subsequently he insisted that the flames merely consumed their natural food.

39

the blind to fondle fish
                    on the boiling surface.
Dogs gnaw the leg bones
                of civilized man.

5

First editor of *The Dial*, Margaret Fuller drowned in a ship-wreck off Fire Island. Emerson asked Thoreau to search for her body.

Margaret Fuller was too smart.
She disapproved my rugged art.
"Too assuming," "badly bred,"
"Give it me again," she said.
        Margaret Fuller is dead.

"I know the men of this countree,
and not a one is match to me.
They're ignorant, vain, easily led,
unsympathetic." That's what she said.
        Now she's dead.

6

Schoolteacher, lecturer, naturalist, land surveyor, he turned a two-week outing into his first moral epic.

His voice trumpeted down the Merrimack,
thundered in the bad Concord air,
"speaking to their condition to make them wince."

"A man does best when he is most himself."

Teacher, he held his hands behind his back;
his lecturer's finger chid, then flicked his hair
from his forehead; he surveyed the Mount of
                             Venus.

The land was his by labor and by measure.
"He who is right is a majority of one."

7

The ants jostle through the pews
toward their love, which burns in Heaven,
entitled *Holy:* The Many and The Few,
an ancient story author Herman
Melville knew but made his captains
sail and resail until the end,
as limp as a fall on a capstan,
flapping on the brass like a severed hand.
The priest who holds the Book of Prayer
mumbles absolution, death
by fire for the sins of air
fanned by an albatross's breath.
Worms and lovers of dark ways
greet death by water: There the font
washes the heart; the skin decays,
cast off by the soul; and plain men plant
complex redemption, stealing colors
from the funky chart of time. That blue
which from the Pacific pours into Walden
Pond becomes a pair of eyes
straining from the cold stone floor
to the face above the Eucharist.
Age, like the wind, howls at the door,
but the believer, kneeling, shakes his fist,
then opens his hand for a cardboard wafer.
In a forest temple there are no pews;

Thoreau told himself
in his Journal that the
effort to lead the life
which a man imagines
will bring unexpected
success.

He believed that a
government always
crucifies Christ.

death is neither later nor safer,
but a lover expresses no heretical views.
Free man devours himself alive
without devil or alternative.

8

False gods! Fear! Fear! Fear!
Stop!

*The Cantos of Ezra
Pound, XLV.*

*Hath no man a painted paradise on his church wall
harpes et luthes
or where virgin receiveth message*
Mr Adams or no
WITH USURA
between the bride and her groom
No!
The sword in the stone
No!

Unjust laws exist; men
must make the law
free, said Thoreau.

War stagnates
commerce falleth apart
estates separate
beds divide
clothes unstitch
bread poisons
Nor even the Indians
smallpoxed
could stand
CONTRA NATURAM
the dead dog on the hearth
the corpse at the table
on the pillow

a gray skull
papered over
with dollar bills.
Disobey.

9

Divine afflatus drove his desperation.
Goodness guided the grant of a house
in return for replanting the forest. The rest
at cost would come by cart from Concord
like Joseph Hosmer and all whom Henry hosted
as the shingles over the cellar shaped
the hut into history's home. Two years;
then Master Ralph motioned his man,
Waldo the creditor won over Walden,
and the writer retreated who had never ranged far,
who had borrowed an axe to begin his building,
who had siphoned a style from the stiff lips
of the nation. Nobody needed that joke.
Fey philosopher of India, foister!

Thoreau's aunt reported that going to see Henry at Walden Pond was one of Concord's first recreations.

10

Aristotle lied. By nature men
are summer friends. The history of slaves
shows that their bank and compass is *to have*:
The sun that gives each figure's fix at noon
takes away the shadow; conceit then says,
Thou art the Form, the earth, thy property.

Courts were made for fair weather, wrote Thoreau, and for very civil cases.

43

Blind as slime mold, all together build
ameboid temples where they pray for grace,
unforethoughtful of the winter wind
which some brisk day will blow their skyscrapers
apart, befouling every place.

Immoral slave who pleads a moral cause,
bankrupt in Heaven and on earth a stone,
man sets his course against the natural laws,
plotting the steps to seize the beautiful
but coming, after all, to his own wet bones.

11

When his first book
was remaindered, he
bought all the copies.

As a trout lurks in a quiet pool
contemplating the surface,
he swung deep inside his soul,
his "most sacred nature,"
conjuring society there,
the reaches of the river,
the unroofed book, the pantheist air,
triumph out of failure:
"I have now a library of nearly nine hundred
                                    volumes,
over seven hundred of which I wrote myself."

The lover humanizes:
the naturalist follows.

"The horses came running, for company I thought."
Bent said I might put it in my book so,
it would do no harm, but in fact they came for salt.
There was some in my pocket, I replied.
Bent said, "That's what they smelt, the salt."

44

12

In the dark corner of the nation
crawling through the shadows cast
by lights from the capitol's dome, an impatient
black man tunnels out of the past
toward the altar of the North Star.

A bad government
makes life less
valuable.

Today John Brown is hanging: Alcott
is reading the Bible; Emerson's part
is the text of the telegram; David
will quote applicable verse, later
dispatch a defense to the memorial
service in the Adirondacks.

The congregation prays for freedom
but cannot compensate its lacks
by making, or by giving the captured Indians,
Christianity and artifacts.

13

The beast will burst from the tin cage.
Its flames will burn the Latin words
of the ground-sniffer, will boil the collyrium
off his agate eyes. Its bared rage
will terrorize the queens of Concord
and drive their white fingers to delirium.

Thoreau met and
admired Whitman,
said that men had
reason to be ashamed
of themselves.

14

La Rivière Longue rises
in the sunset.

He went to Minnesota
in search of health.

Tubercular man aspires
to drink it,
to be purged and repaired
by water,
to cool the room's smoked air
and make the mind shine as
it ought to.

He died of tuber-
culosis and was buried
in Concord's Sleepy
Hollow Cemetery.

Death cuts a hundred lesions
in a lover.
A façade is cracked by collisions
with moving
wishes. Time is power.
His mission
turns cold and sour
who fears the ant's fundamental
passion.

THE BLUE CAT

The Blue Cat

Night is
   a dirty mountain
   flowers drifting on a windless ocean
   wild horses stampeding across a road
   a broken face

 Over the earth's head
its hot coals burning the sky
   a blue cat
    sails
    out of the sunrise

Still Life

In a living room of objets d'art
waiting for death—a faïence jar
from Saint-Porchaire, a della Robbia
Christ-and-Mary in azure myopia,
English foxhounds in a woven scene
leaping across the firescreen—
a footfall cracks the walnut air.

Embroidered ladies on Empire chairs
turn like fish in a stream. The parquet
floor trembles past Chambray.
From the high window through the dirty pane
sunlight screams like a bullet aimed
at the heart of the embalmed world.

Smooth, cold, its ice eyes pearled
by the speckled light, a jade blue cat
swells into life, so exquisite that
the figure beatifies the place.
A mortal cat has a hungry face,
but like a perfect image in a story,
the blue cat bleeds in perfect glory.

The Blue Cat & the Revolution

On the other side of a wall
a tall
blue cat
in a pepper-and-salt tweed hat
is singing a roundelay:
    Serpent plombé, tain de miroir,
    enchanté de vous revoir.

A boy with a gun in hand
takes a stand
too late
at the open city gate
and has nothing to say.
    Instead, the cat: *Whoever you are,*
    enchanté de vous revoir.

A girl with a pen and rule
from school
pauses
to teach the cat the causes
of No Parking signs today.
    The cat: *O folle de désespoir,*
    enchanté de vous revoir.

A porcelain soldier shoots
and loots
the boy
and girl's plastic toy

world. The cat prays:
> *Seigneur, vite! Punis ce soir*
> *les âmes en peine qui veulent Te voir.*

The Great Wall is a screen
between
the sea
and the Himàlayas.
It shines in memory,
which through the cat will say:
> *Ce n'est pas la mer à boire;*
> *enchanté de vous revoir.*

Saints & Trippers

Look: the blue cat climbs the acid trees
   spaced out between his groovy knees,
     the gray-domed vault of limpid vision,
      the sugared teeth, the lips' collision—
      Peace, brother.

Transparencies: his purled eye sees
   her yellow hair strung on the breeze
     like smoke, her ears two cloverleaves
      whorled by the cops' sticks then reeved
      in peace, brother.

His stoned mind floats like vegetables
   down the Seine to Notre Dame in the capital
     of the world. His feelings rise like Bach,
      glass notes tumbling out of rock
      (Peace, brother)

from Gabriel's trumpet in spiral love,
   betrayed by what they're not afraid of:
     Death bled red that alkaline cat;
      overhead hangs his cardinal hat:
      Peace, brother.

Identity Crisis

He was urged to prepare for success: "You never can tell,"
    he was told over and over; "others have made it;
    one dare not presume to predict. You never can tell.

Who's Who in America lists the order of cats
    in hunting, fishing, bird-watching, farming,
    domestic service—the dictionary order of cats

who have made it. Those not in the book are beyond the pale.
    Not to succeed in your chosen profession is unthinkable.
    Either you make it or—you're beyond the pale.

Do you understand?"
                "No," he shakes his head.
    "Are you ready to forage for freedom?"
                              "No," he adds,
    "I mean, why is a cat always shaking his head?

Because he's thinking: who am I? I am not
    only one-ninth of myself. I always am
    all of the selves I have been and will be but am not."

"The normal cat," I tell him, "soon adjusts
    to others and to changing circumstances;
    he makes his way the way he soon adjusts."

"I can't," he says, "perhaps because I'm blue,
    big-footed, lop-eared, socially awkward, impotent,
    and I drink too much, whether because I'm blue

or because I like it, who knows. I want to escape
    at five o'clock into an untouchable world
    where the top is the bottom and everyone wants to escape

from the middle, everyone, every day. I mean,
    I have visions of two green eyes rising
    out of the ocean, blinking, knowing what I mean."

"Never mind the picture, repeat after me
    the self's creed. What he tells you you
    tells me and I repeats. Now, after me:

I love myself, I wish I would live well.
    Your gift of love breaks through my self-defeat.
    All prizes are blue. No cat admits defeat.
The next time that he lives he will live well."

Early Morning in White River Junction

Reality muddles together:
 the phalanxes Ares has charge of
 surrender to Aphrodite's
 electric pomology whether
led on by the sword or the nightie.

Felinity twitches a whisker.
 Coherence applies for addresses.
 A blasphemy opens the window
 to let in Don Juan: cats know where
 their lady is quickly undressing.

A breakfast assignment is special
 if held in the Polka Dot Restaurant.
 Marie is the waitress, and Doris,
 the cook. Bright red mice dance around on
the walls. The hot jukebox tomorrows

the tune of a lay—oh, the piece now
 is grossly inflated. Havana
 cigars lie unwanted. A woman
 of parts expects to be totalled
not beat with a Polish banana.

The cat that is blue tips his hat, true,
 but Anna smiles back from the register.

They make up a pastry of tasteless
   boohoos with a dough once homogeneous.
Bacteria leaven their love. You

whose twenty pink eyes burn the darkness,
   start kissing your floozy and cursing,
   but curtains, I say, to your restaurant
   where love is a whistle or notice,
 a pass at the slip of the solstice

northeast in the frozen direction
   of Iceland. No, here a cat's hopping
   shorts the glass fuse: "Next Selection"
   remains in the rack, needle poised, while
   out back in the bathroom a couple
 are ripping it off without stopping.

Yes, here in the Polka Dot Restaurant
   the pancakes and syrup are sweeter
   than Gilead balm, and the promise
   of finding a cat you can count on
 is more than just reading the comics.

Home Run

Exactly i am
travelling i
see
n. y. c.
see
common toms
Grimes
Napoleonic claws
performances
congresses
ceramics
Gristedes
printemps
today.

Of course, Madam,
travel broadens—
a nuclear opportunity.
In Florence
my companion said
and 1,000
mutinied
on the spot.
How many
tonight
are
dead?

The base angles
of isosceles
triangles
are
180
minus what?
The penultimate Mason
is on the verge
of
freezing
loving
?

Bergman
Rohmer
Buñuel
paaaaah!

Christmas
Provolone
electric snow
you
asleep
yes, you

knock knock
who's
the curtains
the rugs
the chairs
the beds

are
no
who
yes
dead?

Au printemps
ceramics
philately
spark plugs
yes
i am exactly
see
here.
Come in.

The Blue Cat's Daughter

A girl glides by on roller-coaster gloves,
    luscious in the saffron evening air.
      Who wouldn't cut a feather for her hair
swinging like ten pendulums in love?
          Her firefly eyes
          kiss the sky.

That shallop symmetry burst from the hawse
    of her father. Bare-shouldered like the moon, she slats
    upon the local all-night lagoon. Cats
at anchor swing to the truth of her windless cause.
          The lids of her eyes
          batten the sky.

First down, then up: Her petalled body dives
    like a swan with hands into the terrible dawn.
    The darkness ripples on the standard lawn,
then like the tide backs out of the modern drive.
          Her drowned eyes
          sleep in the sky.

The Blue Cat Replies to a Critic

No, Celia, you are wrong to bristle
at my withdrawal. That second whistle,
the one that turned your auburn head
and landed you *dos d'âne* in bed,
was meant for Prue. Your deception
doubled by a false conception,
pull, pull down the wool, rip off the scales,
and write in time a true-life tale.

A passing Persian with gold hair
draws brief attention; her melodic air
evaporates from sight and mind.
A double note, two doublets bind
contentious lovers to one score;
once played, there isn't any more.
Four eyes in rhythm cannot roam
save toward a well-framed common home.

So, let's be frank with one another:
Opponents make the surest brothers.
Saint Agatha protects from quakes,
but holding hands begins with shakes.
A kiss, a verse, a girl's undone—
Sir Whiskers must be on the run.
No, here I stay and, so, propose
you timeless, apodictic prose.

He Foretells His Passing

I can imagine, years from now, your coming back
to this high, old, white house. 'Home' I shouldn't say
because we can't predict who'll live here with a different name.
How tall the birches will be then. Will you look up
from the road past the ash for light in the study windows
upstairs and down? Go climb the black maple as first
in new sneakers you walked forty feet in air
and saw the life to come. Don't forget the cats.

Because you grow away from a house, no matter how much
                                you come back,
if the people you love are elsewhere, or if the reason is, say,
nostalgia, don't worry about small changes or lost names.
Sit down for a minute under the tallest birch. Look up
at the clouds reflected in the red barn's twisted window.
Lean on the wall. Hear our voices as at first
they shook the plaster, laughed, then burned in the dry air
like a wooden house. I imagine you won't forget the cats.

The Blue Cat Rumble

Wearing an afro as big as a bush
   the blue cat told me to blow:
"Ain't nothing you can do around here
   'cept pack your ass and go.
   Ain't no business here
   for cats the color of snow."

His mother was a long-haired whore
   who twice a year at least
persuaded half the local boys
   to do the two-backed beast.
   Not even a Siamese twist
   could make her confess to a priest.

So, who his father is or was
   nobody knows or cares.
I've had charge of this block ten years—
   the spaniels travel in pairs.
   I have a harem of hundreds,
   and none of them puts on airs.

I says to this son of a bitch, I says,
   "Who in hell do you think you are?"
He snakes his tail around his feet,
   his claws cut into the tar;
   he sways his head like a tree
   and shakes like a stone-filled jar.

"You semitic sham, you shipman's hose,
    you moth-eaten fagot of fleas,
I is the word and the light combined,
    and I'm getting rid of these.
    I'm cleaning out the shits,
    like my uncle Hercules."

I shifted right, ready to spring,
    my weight on all four paws,
because in matters of peace-or-war
    you've got to temper the laws
    of thermodynamics and speed
    with modifying claws.

I went for his throat; he went for my rump;
    I went for his two furred balls.
We spun around in a wailing sound
    then fell as an airplane falls
    down a manhole into the sewer,
    the tubular Underground Halls.

The blue cat raised his hand as a sign
    to follow wherever he led.
A beautiful tiger was whoring in back
    with dogs on a dirty bed.
    A Persian was pulling the hypos
    out of its pincushion head.

A hundred kittens were sucking the teats
    of a gargantuan leopardess while

forty black panthers paraded the scene
    and swept everything out of the aisle.
    Before me appeared a fox
    in the latest mini style.

A deacon enjoined a prayer for my soul;
    the fox gave a flick of her tail.
We fused upon the wastes of Hell
    like a solitary sail.
    We rounded up the world,
    then set it, calm and pale,

in revolutionary motion.
    Having changed our planet's
course, we composed a telescopic
    verse with which to scan it.
    But love outspoken dies:
    The selfish readers damned it.

When I awoke the stage was gone,
    the asphalt street was bare.
Vanishing over the rise of the hill
    the blue cat's afro hair
    carried away the hope
    that I could be loved and fair.

"You son of a bitch," I snarled at his back,
    "you ain't changing a thing.
You can stew in the juice of your rotting head
    and suck your tail in a ring.

I'm the boss of this block for good,
    like an old-time English king."

Out of the silence from over the hill
    a haunting laugh replied:
"You mother-fucking, pig-loving cat,
    you're glassy buttons inside.
    You don't mean nothing to me,
    and I got nothing to hide.

"Tomorrow night I'm coming up;
    I'll meet you wherever you are.
And when I'm through I'll have you pickled
    and shown in a 2-lb. jar.
    Then the science boys can prove,
    Baby, that's how things are."

What really gets me, I want to say,
    is not the dogs or the laws
or even the different colors of fur,
    but the similar shapes of claws.
    I'd give up this block, I think,
    if there weren't any wars.

Communicating with the Beyond

Green peppers hang from the purple trees,
 from bruised, barren, autumn bones.
This is the orchard of the Pharisees;
 these are the public telephones.
The blue cat waits, still as clay,
 for the decadal, harmonic grace.

There is the cat with the withered hand:
 What does that sheep cry from the pit?
On the olive hills the gored land
 bleeds, blind and dumb, but the hypocrite
guards his wheat. *Not you, not here*
 reverberates to the Red Sea.

As bitter as burnt almonds is
 the aftertaste of city love.
Streets divide. The house that was His
 lies empty. In the chill air a dove
calls its mate to the south, prays
 her again to play the queen.

Poetomu ja otrekajus',
 convicted of unworthiness,
self-suspicious, hollow of purpose,
 schooled, like a rabbi, to petty business.
I have been in Hell, have seen
 the black fruit on the black trees.

68

The tender bodies in Gehenna burn
     like wet leaves. The stillborn air
muffles the farewells. Concerned
     officials kneel in public prayer:
Anathema Maran atha,
     who will get the beekeeper's job?

Pepper seeds drop from dry mouths. Words
     circle the new electric garden.
Out of the current, commanding the herd,
     comes the voice of the dying warden:
Why have you forsaken me?
     The blue cat shrugs and passes on.

Alone, he now lives on the moon,
     in the gaunt bank of our common sorrow.
He stares down the sun each noon
     and sings to stars that may go out tomorrow.
The music we hear in the azure sky
     is the blue cat's orchestra passing by.